Living Sanely In An Insane World

Living Sanely In An Insane World:
Philosophy For Real People
is part of the
Living Sanely Series.

For more information on forthcoming titles
in this series visit:
www.livingsanely.com.

Living Sanely In An Insane World

PHILOSOPHY
FOR
REAL PEOPLE

John F. Groom

A NOTE ABOUT THESE QUOTES

The inclusion of quotes by others is not intended to imply that any of the parties quoted
agree with or endorse any of the ideas or positions of the author. The quotes are simply
intended to provide thought-provoking context for the topics being discussed.

FIRST EDITION

Published in the United States by Attitude Media

2 4 6 8 10 9 7 5 3 1

Printed in the United States of America

Contents

*In the depth of winter, I finally learned
that within me there lay an invincible summer.*

— ALBERT CAMUS

Living Sanely In An Insane World

The Purpose of Life

*"My philosophy, in essence, is the concept of man as a heroic being,
with his own happiness as the moral purpose of his life,
with productive achievement as his noblest activity,
and reason as his only absolute."*

— AYN RAND
Russian-American philosopher and novelist, 1905–1982

*"Happiness lies in the joy of achievement
and the thrill of creative effort."*

— FRANKLIN D. ROOSEVELT
Thirty-second U. S. President 1882–1945

*"I think the purpose of life is to be useful, to be responsible,
to be honorable, to be compassionate. It is, after all, to matter:
to count, to stand for something, to have made
some difference that you lived at all."*

— LEO C. ROSTEN
American writer, 1908–1977

Insane World

Most people say that they seek happiness, but they don't have a clear idea as to what leads to happiness. They often think that the more money they have, the happier they would be, although they may not have any clear idea as to what they would do with greater wealth. Many others seek happiness through power, prestige, or sensual pleasure.

Living Sanely

The purpose of life is to create value.

Creating value may take many forms. In business, you may produce goods and services that satisfy the needs of others. You can create value by creating art that satisfies only yourself. You can create value by being a good parent, helping the elderly, or by working in a non-profit organization. Many different types of productive work involve progress toward a goal, and, ultimately, the satisfaction of achieving a goal. (Although the progress is usually more rewarding than the satisfaction.)

One may create value as the president of a large corporation, as a small craftsman, working with the needy, helping family members, or in an almost infinite variety of other ways. But simply intending to create value is not enough; results matter:

- The president of a large corporation who increases profitability, while also respecting the need for honesty and candor in dealing with customers, employees, and shareholders, is adding value. The person in the same position who loses money, or who engages in unethical behavior, is destructive.

- Charitable activity may create value by encouraging self-sufficiency, or it may be a hindrance to those one seeks to help.

- A good parent creates value by helping his or her child become a productive, happy person. A bad parent teaches their child destructive values.

- A good philosopher adds value by helping himself and others make intelligent decisions, and see the world in a more comprehensible way. A bad philosopher destroys value by causing confusion and uncertainty and, perhaps even worse, extolling the virtues of confusion. A good philosopher creates value through thoughtful, rational, guidance; a bad philosopher destroys value by discouraging independent thought.

FOCUS

Concentrate your time and energy on those actions, plans, and goals that will create the most value.

Passion and the Purpose of Philosophy

"Most true happiness comes from one's inner life, from the disposition of the mind and soul. Admittedly, a good inner life is hard to achieve, especially in these trying times. It takes reflection and contemplation and self-discipline."

— WILLIAM L. SHIRER
American journalist and historian, 1904–1993

"Seek out that particular mental attribute which makes you feel most deeply and vitally alive, along with which comes the inner voice which says, 'This is the real me,' and when you have found that attitude, follow it."

— WILLIAM JAMES
American philosopher and psychologist, 1842–1910

"I have found that the greatest help in meeting any problem with decency and self-respect and whatever courage is demanded, is to know where you yourself stand. That is, to have in words what you believe and are acting from."

— WILLIAM FAULKNER
American writer, 1897–1962

Insane World

Philosophers demonstrate their mastery and understanding of life by a detached calm; the ideal attitude seems to be that little, if anything, could really matter once one has found the "truth."

Living Sanely

The purpose of philosophy is not to quench passion, but to enhance it. Life is full of surprises, sudden change, hope, and disappointment. Philosophy provides a perspective, and serves as a path and a guide, so that one never loses sight of the goals, even if the insanity of the times causes temporary despair.

Most young people are filled with hopes and dreams. As they encounter obstacles, unfairness, and irrationality, they usually give up or compromise their dreams; daily life becomes grinding, dull, and routine. A sound philosophy should help restore and nurture the spirit of youth as they fight the battles of adulthood.

More than anything else, the purpose of philosophy is to remind you that you are in control of your own life. You can choose your own goals and the rules you use to guide your life. You are accountable only to yourself.

FOCUS

Yesterday is past; now is the time to develop and live by your own philosophy.

God

"True religion is the life we lead, not the creed we profess."

— LOUIS NIZER
American lawyer, 1902–1994

*"Blessed is he who carries within himself a God,
an ideal, and obeys it."*

— LOUIS PASTEUR
French scientist, 1822–1895

*"A beautiful child, only a few weeks old, suddenly dies of a strange
pneumonia in its little bed; cancer or rabies brings anguished death to
the innocent and the needed; normally beneficent fire leaps out in red
anarchy and incinerates a family in the night; earthquakes devastate
Lisbon or San Francisco; pride of power puts the pistol to the heads of
thousands of the noblest sons of Poland in Katyn Forest and tries to
shovel them down under from the knowledge of man; Keats dies,
abandoned by the shallow, futile woman he loved, and seemingly
ignored and lacerated by the men who rule his day; right seems
forever on the scaffold and wrong forever on the throne: How, then,
in such a world, can there be a God both all-powerful and all-good?"*

— E. MERRILL ROOT
American poet, 1895–1973 (For Root, the question above is
rhetorical — he believed in an omnipotent, benevolent God.)

Insane World

People view God, whatever they conceive it to be, as omnipotent and benevolent, and God's creation, people, as obviously flawed. While people fight with one another, and cast endless aspersions on other people, they continue to praise and worship a perfect God.

Yet if the creator is perfect, why is its creation so flawed? Why is life, in its most "natural" state, nasty, brutish, and short, to borrow the famous phrase of Thomas Hobbes. It has taken millions of years of evolution, and an infinite amount of human labor and persistence, to raise mankind from a brutal and primitive existence. Prior to man's development of science and technology, daily life was dominated by hunger, disease, natural disaster, and early death. Most children died before reaching adulthood; the vast majority of human labor was oriented toward the backbreaking and mind-numbing search for the basic necessities of existence. Even in the modern world, the most basic realities have not changed — a newborn baby, without the assistance of other humans, quickly dies. Brutal cold and stifling heat, constant hunger and thirst, an endless variety of health problems — unimproved by man, nature is much closer to resembling Hell than Heaven.

Living Sanely

Perhaps God, or nature, or whatever force is responsible for the creation of humans, is neither omnipotent nor benevolent. Perhaps the force responsible for the creation of mankind is itself terribly flawed, an assumption which might seem very reasonable, given the flawed nature of its human offspring.

People need to see God as a perfect force, in the same way that a young child believes its parents to be perfect. But as people learn more about the complex workings of nature, we might experience the same awakening as a maturing child in regard to its parents — the sense that the creator is neither completely good nor completely evil.

If God is the parent of mankind, perhaps we should model ourselves after the best aspects of the parent and improve its failings. Ultimately, we should surpass our creator, and try to become something that the creator is not — purely good. We would thus rise above the circumstances of our creation, in the same way that each child should try to be a better person than his or her parents.

FOCUS

Rather than battle each other, mankind should be unified by realizing how far we have all come from the terribly difficult and imperfect circumstances of our creation.

The Game

*"One must have the adventurous daring to accept oneself
as a bundle of possibilities and undertake
the most interesting game in the world —
making the most of one's best."*

— HARRY EMERSON FOSDICK
American Protestant minister, 1878–1969

*"The championships, the money, the color; all of these things linger
only in the memory. It is the spirit, the will to excel,
the will to win; these are the things that endure."*

— VINCE LOMBARDI
American football coach, 1913–1970

*"Players must remember that the best victory is
not over the opponent but over oneself."*

— BENJAMIN FRANKLIN
American statesmen and scientist,
commenting on the game of chess, 1706–1790

Insane World

Relatively meaningless sports and games — such as golf, football, and poker — have clearly defined rules and goals, while the truly important activities — work, family life, life in general — have much less clearly defined standards of acceptable behavior. Is cheating okay, or okay if you get away with it? What constitutes victory? Wealth? Fame? The love of your family?

Living Sanely

Life really is a game, although a much more complex, difficult, and significant one than those played by athletes. To look at life as a game or sport may help you to set goals, and decide what trade-offs to make. Most importantly, a game mentality may help you adhere strictly to the rules you set for yourself. If your goal is to run a mile in six minutes or less, you know it would be silly, and only cheating yourself, to run three-quarters of a mile in six minutes and tell yourself you had accomplished your goal. Game-thinking encourages honesty with yourself, which is critical to the creation of value and leading a fulfilling life.

In sports and games, there are well-defined rules that all participants agree to abide by. And herein lies the greatest difference between the game of life and trivial games; when you play the great game, you must make your own goals, set your own rules according to your own values, and be your own referee. You keep score for yourself, and, in the end, you are the only one who can decide if you have won or lost.

For some people, climbing Mt. Everest, the world's tallest mountain, is the goal: for others, sailing a boat across the

Atlantic. As challenging as these goals may be, they are not nearly as challenging as making your whole life a game: establishing the goals, setting the rules, and then seeking to win. But you must win on your own terms. As a device for abiding by your own rules, you may find it helpful to compare your goal to something easily defined, such as climbing a mountain or running a marathon.

FOCUS

On life as the longest, most challenging, most comprehensive, and most important game in the world.

Keeping Score

*"There is nothing noble in being superior to some other man.
The true nobility is in being superior to your previous self."*

— HINDU PROVERB

*"You can stand tall without standing on someone.
You can be a victor without having victims."*

— HARRIET WOODS
American politician, 1927–NA

*"There is only one real failure in life that is possible,
and that is, not to be true to the best one knows."*

— JOHN FARRAR
Australian composer, 1945–NA

Insane World

We assess every facet of our lives in comparison to others. Do I make more or less money than my peers? Do I live in a smaller or bigger house than my parents or siblings? Do I have a more important job than the people I went to school with? Am I in better physical shape than my friends? Are my children as successful as my friends' children?

There are a number of problems with keeping score in this way:

- Being more "successful" than those to whom you compare yourself may not make you happy.

- People have completely different advantages and "starting points." If you are in the race for wealth, you may be at quite a disadvantage competing against someone who has inherited a vast fortune. In every respect — beauty, intelligence, athletic ability — people have widely varying inheritances.

- There will always be others who are more successful than you in some way, thus it may be impossible to win the game; this fact may lead you to feel bitter. Conversely, there will always be those who are not as successful as yourself, perhaps leading you to arrogance or conceit.

- You have no control over the actions of others. Thus, no matter how hard you try, you may lose the game. And just the fact of not having control may be frustrating.

- Those whom you are competing against may play by a completely different set of rules; it is very frustrating to play a game against those who use different rules.

- Competition with others implies that for some to win, others must lose. This is neither healthy nor true. In fact, when an individual creates value, many people benefit.

Living Sanely

Once you've determined how you will create value, decide how you will keep track of that value — that is your way of keeping score. And remember that the game is with yourself, not others. This outlook has a number of very important advantages:

- While you have little or no control over the actions of others, you have almost complete control over your own actions. It is true that there are some events over which you have no control; your plane may crash, you may develop cancer — but overall, on a day-to-day basis, you have a very high degree of control, and complete control over the choices you make. Each day you can decide what you will try to accomplish; each day you can make a full effort, or not. Only you can decide how hard you will work to achieve your goals.

- You can make your own rules and prioritize your values.

- You can score yourself only on those aspects of your life which you believe will lead you to happiness. Perhaps you already have enough money to meet your needs, and you decide that raising happy children is the way that you enjoy creating value. If so, you can focus on your children, and not worry whether your income is keeping pace with others. But if you decide to focus on your children, you should also avoid comparisons in this area. What matters is whether your children are as happy as possible; not whether they're as happy as someone else's children.

FOCUS

Don't compare yourself to others;
focus on improving yourself and your own situation.

Means and Ends

"Let no man turn aside, ever so slightly,
from the broad path of honour, on the plausible pretence
that he is justified by the goodness of his end.
All good ends can be worked out by good means."

— CHARLES DICKENS
English novelist, 1812–1870

"A shortcut to riches is to subtract from one's desires."

— PLUTARCH
Greek writer, 46–120

"The end cannot justify the means for the simple and obvious reason
that the means employed determine the nature of the ends produced."

— ALDOUS HUXLEY
English novelist, 1894–1963

Insane World

The ends justify the means.

What matters is not how you achieve something, but what is achieved. For instance, lying may be permissible if you accomplish some worthwhile goal by lying. Taken to its logical conclusion, as many rulers such as Hitler, Mao, and Stalin have done, even the murder of millions of people may be acceptable in order to achieve some end.

Most people, especially the best people, have an innate inclination to govern their lives by some set of moral rules. But they never really clearly define those rules, and violate the rules when they find it inconvenient to live by them. Thus their life is a muddled conflict between their desire to achieve their goals at all costs, and their desire to act ethically.

Living Sanely

The means justify the ends.

Once you determine your rules, you should learn to accept whatever results accrue from living life according to those rules. For instance, if lying isn't permissible, you must learn to accept the consequences of honesty.

Your rules are for your own benefit; you may wish that others live by the same set of rules, but you have power only over your own actions, not over the actions of others. The rules serve a completely selfish purpose: to make your own life more rewarding, and thus it is, to some extent, irrelevant as to whether others live by your rules of conduct. (Although you may find life most rewarding if, to the degree possible, you seek interaction with those who share your values and abide by a similar set of rules.)

It's not that end results don't matter — they do — or that you should be equally happy with any results as long as you live ethically. You may be quite unhappy with the results, at least in the short term. The decision to live by a certain set of ethical rules is simply to say that in the overall context of life, end results only have value if they are achieved in a morally acceptable way. It is the process, the means, that determines the value of any end.

FOCUS

On the process of creating value,
rather than short-term results.

Money

"Money will give you the means for the satisfaction of your desires, but it will not provide you with desires."

— AYN RAND
Russian-American philosopher and novelist, 1905–1982

"Wealth still failed to impress him; the purpose of money was to purchase one's freedom to pursue that which was useful and interesting."

— H. W. BRANDS
Biographer, describing Benjamin Franklin's attitude toward money

"To fulfill a dream, to be allowed to sweat over lonely labor, to be given a chance to create, is the meat and potatoes of life. The money is the gravy."

— BETTE DAVIS
American actress, 1908–1989

Insane World

The acquisition of money is the ruling passion of our times; most people believe it holds the key to happiness. The ethics of acquiring money vary widely, ranging from those who are willing to do anything to become rich, to those who have some vague but serious notions as to right and wrong ways of becoming wealthy. Methods of acquiring wealth vary from honorable (developing an important business), to lucky (winning the lottery), to sleazy (outrageous lawsuits), to simple theft.

More than any other factor, the unprincipled pursuit of wealth leads to mental and moral confusion, and to the conclusion that we live in an insane world. If the ultimate goal, happiness, depends on which ticket is drawn in a lottery, or what irrational verdict a jury may pronounce, then reason and other critical values like hard work, persistence, and honesty, have less than overwhelming importance. And if we are dependent on luck or the whims of others then we have no control over our destiny.

People seem to pursue wealth for two reasons:

- Keeping score — Many people use money to compare themselves to others: to keep track of their relative success according to whether they have more or less wealth than their peers.

- To enjoy luxury and leisure — Many people dream of endless leisure, but it seems that few people are happy living such a life; people seem to need to have some goals; some productive activity. To be truly happy, people need to create value.

Living Sanely

Money is an important and excellent possession. It enables one to buy whatever can be bought, and many things of great value — leisure, some sensual pleasures, material goods, travel — can be bought. Money can also be used to build a business or to provide assistance to those who need help. But the almost unlimited number of people who are both wealthy and unhappy shows that money is only part of the equation.

To value money, it makes more sense to think of competing types of good, rather than good vs. evil. While money is good, and serves many useful purposes, it is not sufficient for happiness. In order to be content and at peace, one must actively create value and maintain a sense of personal integrity. In a just society, money will be one of the rewards for honestly creating value.

People who obtain wealth without creating value may experience various forms of pleasure, but they will never have a sense of personal fulfillment. People who are striving for the most that life has to offer may hope for wealth. But in the many potential conflicts between integrity, the desire to create value, and money, they should choose the first two at the expense of the latter. Wealth is a question of degree; some is better than none, and there could always be more. Questions of integrity are binary: When properly understood, even very complex issues usually have morally right and wrong responses. Wrong actions are not half wrong, they are simply wrong. Wealth can be made, lost, and made again, but lost integrity is usually not regained.

FOCUS

Money is a tool of exchange. Earn money by fulfilling your highest potential — trade that money for the highest values, and the best products and services that others can create.

Materialism

"The happy people are those who are producing something;
the bored people are those who
are consuming much and producing nothing."

— WILLIAM RALPH INGE
English theologian, 1860–1954

"I was part of that strange race of people aptly described as spending
their lives doing things they detest to make money they don't want to
buy things they don't need to impress people they dislike."

— EMILE HENRY GAUVREAY

"No pleasure philosophy, no sensuality, no place nor power,
no material success can for a moment give such
inner satisfaction as the sense of living for good purposes,
for maintenance of integrity,
for the preservation of self-approval."

— MINOT SIMONS
American Unitarian minister, twentieth century

Insane World

A large house requires extensive furnishings; the extensive grounds require upkeep. Beautiful, exotic cars require maintenance, but not nearly as much as a boat. A designer wardrobe requires cleaning and storage. All purchases require some thought: How much should I pay? What are the tax consequences? Is this a good investment? Does it need to be insured? The more things one has, the more thought they require, and it's easy to lose your freedom of spirit and the ability to focus on the most important things in life, which aren't things. And so often material objects are simply expensive toys, designed to impress others and having little real value to the owner.

Living Sanely

Once you have created value in some form, you have earned the privilege of consuming value in other forms; one of those forms is the possession of material goods. Each new acquisition should be considered carefully, as purchases have a price beyond money. Be like the gourmet, who carefully chooses each dish, rather than the gourmand, who devours everything. I am not arguing for a monastic lifestyle; simply a rigorous discipline. It's not because material possessions are bad, but rather because they are often very good, that it's easy to lose one's focus.

As a producer, the object is to create value, both for others and yourself. As a consumer, your only object is to provide value directly for yourself, or, indirectly, by acting on behalf of others. When considering a purchase ask, "Will this really provide value to me?" "In what way?" An expensive car may be an object of great beauty and style, and provide you with esthetic value. But do you need two such cars? Are you going to be comfortable in a big house, or are you really buying it to impress your friends? If the latter, is impressing your friends a value worth seeking? Does the expensive wine taste better than the inexpensive wine? Can you really tell the difference? As in all things, the difference between pride and vanity is critical — are your purchases designed to bring you pleasure or to impress others?

A wise policy may be to seek only material goods that have a special value to you. A book lover might have a beautiful library filled with expensive rare editions and drive a simple, inexpensive car. Almost everyone can derive some pleasure from material goods, often from the admiration of a well-made or beautiful object. But anyone of intelligence will have higher goals related to work or pleasure. By limiting consumption, one retains the ability to focus on more important goals and activities.

FOCUS

On keeping your life simple by seeking only those material objects which will truly add value to your lifestyle.

Work and Business

*"Far and away the best prize that life offers is the chance
to work hard at work worth doing."*

— THEODORE ROOSEVELT
Twenty-sixth U.S. President, 1858–1919

*"A musician must make music, an artist must paint,
a poet must write, if he is to be ultimately at peace with himself.
What a man can be, he must be."*

— ABRAHAM MASLOW
American psychologist, 1908–1970

*"Being forced to work, and forced to do your best,
will breed in you temperance and self-control,
diligence and strength of will, cheerfulness and content,
and a hundred virtues which the idle never know."*

— CHARLES KINGSLEY
English clergyman and novelist, 1819–1875

Insane World

Most people work, in one form or the other, yet the great majority of those people would rather be doing something else. People seek satisfaction in a wide variety of constructive and destructive activities — drugs and alcohol, the pursuit of sex, travel, sports – but they would usually like to avoid the activity most likely to lead to long-term satisfaction.

Living Sanely

Work is the activity most conducive to living sanely in an insane world. In this case, I'm referring not to the broader concept of creating value, but to economically rewarded work. One can create great value, such as a work of art or happy children, without knowing or caring about the economic consequences of that activity.

Business, on the other hand, requires a focus on economic results. At its best, business provides the opportunity to produce work in which you can take great pride. In return for giving the best of yourself, you hope to receive the highest possible economic rewards. Merging economic drive with pride of product is a great challenge, often resulting in great conflict. It is this combination of challenge and conflict that provides the discipline, focus, and intellectual integration that is very difficult to find outside of work.

Business people often forsake pride for money, in large part because pride is intangible while money is easily quantified, and thus may seem more real. But if work is a central, defining force in life — and it is, as it represents the way most people spend most of their time — anyone who chooses money over pride has defined themselves as someone whose "best" is not noble, nor important. However, in the real world of day-to-day business, some compromise between pride and money is often both necessary and desirable. Ethical compromise, on the other hand, is unacceptable. Economics and pride of product are both matters of degree that involve striving towards ideals; ethics is a matter of binary absolutes.

FOCUS

On developing a career that balances your economic needs with your need to create value and to take pride in your work.

Investing

"The greatest achievement of the human spirit is to live up to one's opportunities, and to make the most of one's resources."

— LUC DE CLAPIERS, MARQUIS DE VAUVENARGUES
French essayist, 1715–1747

"Rely on the ordinary virtues that intelligent, balanced human beings have relied on for centuries: common sense, thrift, realistic expectations, patience, and perseverance."

— JOHN C. BOGLE
American founder of Vanguard Investment Group, 1929–NA

"Now, speculation — in which the focus is not on what an asset will produce but on what the next fellow will pay for it — is neither illegal, immoral, nor un-American. But it is not a game in which Charlie and I wish to play. We bring nothing to the party, so why should we expect to take anything home?"

— WARREN BUFFETT
American investor, alluding to why he and
his partner avoid speculation, 1930–NA

Insane World

People often reserve rational and careful thinking for their business or investment decisions, and think in an entirely different way in other aspects of their lives. But simply because one seeks to maximize intangibles — honor, pride — whatever they may be, does not mean that one has to pursue these values in some sort of irrational, poorly defined way.

Living Sanely

The more intangible the goal, the more it requires clear, hard-headed thinking, and financial investment criteria are excellent for this purpose. One might make an investment, financial or otherwise, in helping a child, or feeding a hungry animal. The idea of return is relevant to all aspects of life; every investment should have a return, although the best return for many investments is a sense of personal satisfaction. And it's sometimes necessary to take losses — to surrender a battle to avoid losing the war — both with people and with business investments.

Greed is wanting more than you have a right to expect, whether the subject is financial investment or life. Since living sanely is most fundamentally about creating value, the first question to ask when making an investment is what value you're adding, and based on that value, what return you should expect. Adding value can take all sorts of forms: money, insight, experience, judgment, courage. The sorts of things that make one a good investor are not very different than the sorts of things which make one a good person.

Some of the most important philosophical elements of

investing, especially independence of judgment, are important to living sanely. Making decisions about what is valuable, and what is not, is fundamental to living well. The most important difference between the investment arena and the broader arena of life is that in the former, all returns are measured financially; whereas in the latter, financial returns are only one part, and not the most important part, of the equation.

FOCUS

On applying rigorous analysis about investment and returns to all aspects of your life.

Heroism, Bravery, and Glory

*"Real heroes are men who fall and fail and are flawed,
but win out in the end because they've stayed true
to their ideals and beliefs and commitments."*

— KEVIN COSTNER
American actor, 1955–NA

*"Man's greatest actions are performed in minor struggles.
Life, misfortune, isolation, abandonment, and poverty
are battlefields which have their heroes —
obscure heroes who are at times greater than illustrious heroes."*

— VICTOR HUGO
French writer, 1802–1885

*"The real glory is being knocked to your knees and then coming back.
That's real glory. That's the essence of it."*

— VINCE LOMBARDI
American football coach, 1913–1970

Insane World

The concepts "bravery" and "glory" seem outdated, appropriate to a different time. Perhaps that's why the word "hero" can cause a tinge of embarrassment. When we think of bravery, we envision soldiers storming the beaches of Normandy in World War II, or explorers trying to find the source of the Nile. Heroism, traditionally defined, seems to require war, disaster, emergency, or uncharted territories.

Given that the traditional opportunities to display bravery have diminished in the modern world, we settle for poor proxies. Actors, such as the late John Wayne, engage in heroism from the safety of a movie set; athletes' on-the-field bravery is limited to a couple of hours every week, scheduled around network advertising.

Living Sanely

The idea of heroism needs to be redefined to fit the realities of modern life. The natural human desire to distinguish oneself through noble action is as strong as ever, but perhaps our criteria for defining what constitutes heroism has always been flawed. Heroism is really the quest to live according to one's internal standards of right and wrong, regardless of whether the world is watching.

Rather than using the dramatic standards of the past, which recognized loud, public and often violent action, the following are criteria for heroism more appropriate to the realities of modern life:

- Heroic action should have some noble and grand intention, but such intention does not need to be altruistic. To build a great and worthwhile business can be a heroic endeavor.

- Heroic deeds and actions must be based on the principle of consent, especially in terms of financing. Many people strive for the rewards of engaging in great ventures, but finance those ventures with money obtained by force. Politicians are especially guilty in this regard, financing grandiose projects with money extorted from unwilling taxpayers. To meet the highest standards of heroism, every part of an action or project must follow consistent ethical standards, one of which is the principle of consent. Many people talk of the great things they could do if only they had the money, but part of doing a great thing is finding an honorable way to pay for it.

- The action brings out the best in people: both the best in the hero, and the best in others. Heroic action appeals to people's highest, most noble feelings. This is especially true in business; it's a much more worthy — and difficult — endeavor to build a business that caters to customers' noble aspirations than to a lowest common denominator.

- The more private the action, perhaps the more heroic. Private action is motivated by the desire to do the right thing, rather than the desire for public acclaim.

- The longer something takes to accomplish, the more heroic the accomplishment. Modern drama is often cast in the form of a sporting event lasting several hours, or a dramatic rescue. But the real test is how long a man or woman can maintain their values in the face of adversity. To believe in something long enough to act, even to risk life and limb, for several hours is one thing, but to have the steadiness and profound belief required to maintain a course of action over years is an entirely different matter.

• As has always been the case, the greater the odds against success, the more heroic the endeavor.

Two other important points:

• Heroism does not always require success; there are many examples of heroic failures. Heroism is more about means than ends, more about process than results.

• Heroes don't need to be perfect: many grand things are done by very flawed persons, and the flaws of the hero don't diminish the grandness of the heroic action. Imperfections in the hero may inspire ordinary people to reach for extraordinary goals.

FOCUS

On the private and quiet, but nonetheless heroic, drama of creating value.

Pride

"It is some fundamental certainty which a noble soul has about itself, something which is not to be sought, is not to be found, and perhaps, also, is not to be lost. The noble soul has reverence for itself."

— FRIEDRICH NIETZSCHE
German philosopher, 1844–1900

"There is overwhelming evidence that the higher the level of self-esteem, the more likely one will be to treat others with respect, kindness, and generosity."

— NATHANIEL BRANDEN
American psychologist, living

"Never be haughty to the humble; never be humble to the haughty."

— JEFFERSON DAVIS
President of the Confederacy during the
American Civil War, 1808–1889

Insane World

Pride is often regarded as either a sin, in religious terms, or as undesirable conceit, in secular terms. "Pride goeth before a fall" is a common platitude. Pride is often contrasted with the virtue of humility.

Living Sanely

Pride is a way you think about yourself, as opposed to vanity, which is a concern with what others think about you. Pride is really the same as self-respect, and both are about substance — what you know to be true, while vanity is about appearances — what appears to be true to other people. Pride is the ultimate bedrock of staying sane in an insane world, because your opinion of yourself is the most important reason to adhere to your own vision of right and wrong. The reward — sometimes the only reward — for doing the right thing, especially in an insane world, is a reinforcement of self-respect.

Pride is what keeps you doing the right thing when no one is looking, and what keeps you trying when you might be tempted to give up. You're in complete control of self-respect, which depends only on your own actions; you have far less control in matters of vanity, because you can't control how others perceive you.

Pride should never be manifested as arrogance. Pride is a private emotion; arrogance is the public display of vanity. The people with the deepest sense of pride are often kind and humble in their interaction with others.

FOCUS

On being proud, not vain.

Uniqueness

"All I would tell people is to hold onto what was individual about themselves, not to allow their ambition for success to cause them to try to imitate the success of others. You've got to find it on your own terms."

— HARRISON FORD
American actor, 1942–NA

"This above all, to thine own self be true, and it must follow, as the night the day, thou canst not then be false to any man."

— WILLIAM SHAKESPEARE
English playwright and poet, 1564–1616

*"If a man does not keep pace with his companions, perhaps it is because he hears a different drummer.
Let him step to the music he hears,
however measured or far away."*

— HENRY DAVID THOREAU
American philosopher and writer, 1817–1862

Insane World

People seek to be unique in superficial, unproductive, and sometimes painful ways. The most common way in which people seek to stand out is with displays of material goods: a large house, expensive cars, and stylish clothes are typical examples. Memberships to exclusive groups — country clubs, fraternities, MENSA, gangs — can provide both a feeling of belonging and uniqueness. Young people are especially likely to resort to drastic methods such as body piercing and tattoos to "mark" themselves as different.

Living Sanely

The search for uniqueness is a natural, good, and important part of being human. Uniqueness can be demonstrated in substantial or trivial ways. Most people wish to be seen as special or different in the eyes of others; some people also wish to prove to themselves that they have unusual talents or other attributes that make them stand out among the crowd.

There are a number of ways in which one can distinguish oneself in a substantial manner: achievement, kindness, character, hard work, and endurance are a few. The fundamental distinguishing characteristic of these attributes is that they are nontransferable; you can give another person your car, your house, or your clothes, but you cannot give them your character or your work ethic.

The most important way an individual can develop uniqueness is the way they create value. There are an infinite number of ways of creating value, and each person has unique capabilities to achieve their goals. One person may seek to create great art; another may develop a small business; another may raise a family, but there are an endless number of different ways of achieving these goals. We may both seek to raise happy, productive children, but we may have completely different methods of achieving that goal. You may believe that firm discipline is the key; I may believe that tolerance is paramount. Uniqueness is demonstrated both by what you seek to achieve, and how you reach that goal.

FOCUS

*On becoming unique in substantial ways
that help you to create value.*

Sex

*"The sexual embrace can only be compared
with music and with prayer."*

— HAVELOCK ELLIS
English sexologist, 1859–1939

*"The life and love of the body is a noble thing,
against which the intellect and the spirit need not wage war."*

— MICHELE ROBERTS
English novelist

*"Morality in sexual relations, when it is free from superstition,
consists essentially in respect for the other person,
and unwillingness to use that person solely as a means of
personal gratification, without regard to his or her desires."*

— BERTRAND RUSSELL
English philosopher and mathematician, 1872–1970

Insane World

Many, perhaps most, people who are married are bored and sexually dissatisfied, leading many of them to have affairs outside of marriage. Both inside and outside of marriage, couples often have unplanned children. Sexually transmitted diseases are widespread. Rape, perhaps the ultimate denial of personal liberty, is far too common.

Living Sanely

Lust is basically a good and powerful force, if enough self-control is maintained to follow these rules:

- Adult consent: Your partner must consent without threat of physical force, and must understand the act to which they are consenting. Rape should be brutally punished.

- Honor the vows: One of the principal tenets of living sanely is the importance of honoring commitments and fulfilling contracts. Sometimes the best way of doing this is simply not to make commitments. For some people, marriage is the best path; if spouses swear sexual fidelity, they should honor that oath. People should make whatever arrangements are most suitable for them, perhaps including variations of the traditional marriage contract. But they should honor whatever agreement they enter into.

- Planned parenthood: To bring a new life into the world is the most profound thing a person can do. If children are produced, the creators of the children — the parents — have a very serious obligation to care for those children. If children are not intended, birth control should be used. Sane people don't rely on "luck" to protect them from committing a great mistake.

- Protect the body: You should protect your own body, as well as the body of your sexual partner, from sexually transmitted disease.

Prostitution is a difficult issue. Women who sell their bodies to men are regarded as prostitutes, and condemned, if they prostitute themselves to different men. However, to marry primarily for wealth – to prostitute yourself to a single man or woman — is socially accepted. On the one hand, a choice by a man or woman to sell themselves seems very wrong, and clients are only encouraging this wrong choice when they hire a prostitute.

On the other hand, prostitution is, in many ways, a very honest act. Unlike much dating or "romance," there is no pretense that the transaction is about anything other than the physical act of sex. The seller, usually a woman, offers to rent her body for a limited time to the buyer, usually a man. Typically, the transaction occurs without either force or fraud, and both parties receive what they sought — payment for the prostitute and a sexual experience for the client. Perhaps the greatest problem with prostitution is that it degrades sexuality by treating sex as primarily a physical, rather than a spiritual, act.

FOCUS

Lust is a great and positive force, as long as you obtain the consent of your adult partner, protect your body, honor your commitments, and avoid unplanned children.

Sex and Materialism

"Beauty in things exists in the mind which contemplates them."

— DAVID HUME
Scottish philosopher and historian, 1711–1776

"Sex is emotion in motion."

— MAE WEST
American actress, 1893–1980

*"The flesh is suffused by the spirit, and it is forgetting
this in the act of love-making that
creates cynicism and despair."*

— MAY SARTON
American writer, 1912–1995

Insane World

Sex is either regarded as something that is basically evil and should be yielded to reluctantly, or something that is good and should be pursued enthusiastically, with the latter position gaining acceptance over time. But in either case, sex is viewed as an animal instinct, and primarily a physical experience. Nothing could be further from the truth; the actual experience of sexuality depends to a large extent on perception. The focus on sex as a physical rather than spiritual experience has led many physically attractive people to spend a great deal of time and energy unsuccessfully searching for satisfying sexual experiences.

Living Sanely

The experience of sex has as much to do with the mind as with the body.

Imagine that you are blindfolded and forced to have sex, in silence, with an unidentified person. Could you tell whether that person had a beautiful or ugly face? What could you know about the person's skin tone? Could you determine the color of their hair? Perhaps you could tell, in a very crude way, something about the shape of their body, but far less than if you had your vision restored. From your blindfolded sexual experience you could tell little or nothing about their day-to-day personality, whether they were generally promiscuous or chaste, or any other aspect of their character.

All in all, you could not assess any of the factors that would normally lead you to determine whether someone was sexually attractive. Yet, the act itself, the physical motions of copulating, would be the same as if you had all that knowledge. The knowledge of who you are having sex with is a critical ingredient of your sexual experience, yet this knowledge has little or nothing to do with the physical act of sex.

Even in the case of sex in its crudest form, prostitution, seemingly devoid of the spiritual element, the appearance of the prostitute is very important to the client. On the other hand, the appearance of the client may not matter to the prostitute, and this is the point at which sex has become a purely physical, mechanical act. And the point at which it becomes a purely physical act is the point at which it is boring and meaningless to the participant. When the sexual act becomes purely physical, its primary value is outside of the act itself, such as earning money (for the prostitute), satisfying a marital obligation, or proving virility.

Another example that shows how the experience of sex is primarily in the mind is sexual repetition. For many, especially men, the sexual experience is much more interesting and important the first time one has sex with a particular individual. Over time, the experience may change from being dramatic and exciting to routine and trivial, even if one's lover has not physically changed at all over time. If sex is primarily a physical event, it should make no difference whether one has had sex with a partner once or a thousand times. Yet we find that the only couples that seem to maintain a rewarding long-term sexual relationship are those that maintain a deep emotional interest in each other.

If sex is primarily a physical act, it should make no difference whether your partner enjoyed his or her participation, or whether the partner was bored, angry, sweet, inviting, or aloof. Yet the attitude of one's partner clearly does affect the sexual experience.

FOCUS

On sex as a spiritual experience.

Marriage

"It is mind, not body, that makes marriage last."

— PUBLILIUS SYRUS
Roman writer, first century B.C.

"He that marries for wealth sells his liberty."

— GEORGE HERBERT
English religious poet, 1593–1633

*"Many a marriage hardly differs from prostitution,
except being harder to escape from."*

— BERTRAND RUSSELL
English philosopher and mathematician, 1872–1970

Insane World

People vow to live with each other for the rest of their lives, giving little thought to whether, in the long run, marriage really makes sense. Not surprisingly, most marriages end in divorce or disappointment. People select a mate based to a large extent on physical attraction, yet physical attraction is only a small part of what is necessary to sustain a long-term, day-to-day relationship.

Most people do not have the virtues necessary to sustain a happy marriage. Intelligence, a variety of interests, a sense of humor, character — all these abstractions become quite real when living with someone day-to-day. Put simply, marriages cannot be any better than the people who are married.

Despite omnipresent evidence about the difficulties inherent in marriage, most people still get married. For those who intend to have children, this makes great sense, as children need two parents: The marriage vow indicates the agreement, or at least intention, of husband and wife to stay together and fulfill their role as parents.

What accounts for the continuing attraction of marriage, even among those who don't intend to have children? Some would cite the influence of family, morality, or religion. But I believe an additional force is important — the desire to create the illusion of permanence in an impermanent world. Many people believe that the legalities and formalities of the marriage ceremony make their relationship more permanent. This may be true from a legal standpoint, but no ceremony can permanently bind people's affection, or attraction, to each other. In fact, the illusion of a binding tie may have the opposite result, by lessening the incentive to be attractive, physically or otherwise, to their mates.

Living Sanely

Marriage creates legal and/or religious bonds, but it can't create the bonds that will make for a happy partnership between two people. As in any other situation, potential participants should ask themselves how the institution of marriage will help them create value. Far too often, marriage is motivated by economic interest. If people seek to create economic partnerships, they should do so without cloaking those arrangements in the language of love. However, even if the romantic tie is genuine and strong, the expectations of each partner in the marriage should be clearly defined; love is not an excuse to be foolish.

For those who simply seek romance and companionship, there is little reason to marry. If the objective is to raise children, this should be agreed on prior to marriage. As in all things, honesty should be foremost; each party should be clear as to their expectations. The institution of marriage can help people create value, if both parties clearly define their expectations. For instance, marriage can provide the structure and discipline some people need to enhance a permanent relationship. Most importantly, marriage can define each party's responsibilities in the ultimate act of value creation — the creation of a family. Marriage is important not only in starting a family, but in helping to define relationships within the extended family.

FOCUS

Will marriage help lovers create value?

Parenthood

"Children need models rather than critics."

— JOSEPH JOUBERT
French philosopher, 1754–1824

*"The most important thing a father can do for
his children is to love their mother."*

— THEODORE HESBURGH
American, former president of
Notre Dame University, 1917–NA

*"Some people seem compelled by unkind fate
to parental servitude for life."*

— SAMUEL BUTLER
English writer, 1835–1902

Insane World

As has sadly always been the case, many children are neglected or even abused. But there is a phenomenon that is unique to modern life: parents who devote too much, rather than too little, time and effort to their children. The lives of these parents revolve around their children, leading their children to assume that it is the obligation of those around them to cater to their every whim. Parents equate "being a good parent" with living for their children.

Living Sanely

While a great deal of stress, aggravation, and drudgery is an unavoidable part of being a parent, on balance, parenthood should be more pleasure than pain. Parents should provide guidance and rules, as well as moral, emotional, and financial support – but not entertainment. Many children have discovered future joys, such as serious reading, as a result of being forced to entertain themselves.

The great majority of successful adults did not have "perfect" childhoods, if such a thing is possible. Not attending private schools, poor athletic ability, or trouble with peers are not tragedies. Childhood is supposed to train a person to be an adult, which means learning to deal with problems and an imperfect world.

Three important things you can do for your child are:

- Help them to develop a philosophy of life that addresses the unfairness — and the general irrationality and insanity — they are bound to encounter.

- Help them to discover ways that they enjoy creating value.

- Help them develop the habit of focusing on improving their own life, rather than comparing themselves to others.

FOCUS

On helping your children to learn to entertain themselves and to view problems as interesting challenges.

The Human Body

"The body is the soul's image; therefore keep it pure."

— SIXTUS I
Pope of the Roman Catholic Church from 115–125

"If anything is sacred, the human body is sacred."

— WALT WHITMAN
American poet, 1819–1892

*"A good sweat, with the blood pounding through my body,
makes me feel alive, revitalized. I gain a sense of mastery
and assurance. I feel good about myself.
Then I can feel good about others."*

— ARTHUR DOBRIN
American ethicist and writer, 1943–NA

Insane World

Huge numbers of people seem to fall into one of two undesirable categories. Those in the first group don't take care of their bodies and, as a result, these people are often overweight and/or in poor health. Those in the second group are very concerned about their appearance, and employ artificial means, including bizarre diets, drugs, and plastic surgery, to improve their looks. Those in the first group look and feel bad; the members of the second group look, and are, artificial. I'm not sure which is worse.

Living Sanely

Maintaining your health and improving your appearance are ways of creating value. You should strive to improve your physical health and appearance in accordance with your priorities. For some people, staying in top physical shape is one of their primary ways of creating value, and they will be willing to devote large amounts of time and energy to exercise. Others may only be willing to devote the minimal amount of time necessary to maintain adequate physical health, with no concern for their appearance. Either approach, or anything in between, may be valid.

The following two rules of living sanely are especially relevant to issues of health and appearance:

- Don't compare yourself to others.

- Be honest.

Rule number one means that you make the most of your own

health and appearance, without reference to others. To the extent that you are willing to devote time and energy to improving your appearance, your standard of improvement should be yourself, not others. For example, if you exercise by running, you might focus on improving your speed, not on comparing yourself with how fast someone else runs, which is irrelevant.

The most important principal of living sanely is honesty. Cosmetic surgery that enlarges some portion of a person's body by filling it with plastic is a fundamental lie; they are trying to appear to be something they are not. An honest person accepts the natural framework of their body, and makes the most of it – naturally.

Just as keeping score in business requires playing by certain rules, rules apply to your appearance and your body. In both business and fitness, the purpose of the rules is the same: to provide the discipline and framework in which you, rather than someone else, creates value. If your body is beautiful because of drugs or plastic surgery, it's the chemist or surgeon who has created that value. If you make your body beautiful through exercise, you have created value — something of which you can be proud.

FOCUS

On exercise and diet as honest ways of creating value through improved health and appearance.

Science and Technology

"Technologies are the cart before the horse. It's wonderful to have all these whiz-bang gadgets if you know what to do with them. Gadgets for the sake of gadgets, which I think a lot of this computer technology is, isn't going to help you."

— STEPHEN LEEB
American investor and author, living

"The means by which we live have outdistanced the ends for which we live. Our scientific power has outrun our spiritual power. We have guided missiles and misguided men."

— MARTIN LUTHER KING, JR.
American civil rights leader, 1929–1968

"Our inventions are wont to be pretty toys, which distract our attention from serious things. They are but an improved means to an unimproved end."

— HENRY DAVID THOREAU
American philosopher and writer, 1817–1862

Insane World

Science and technology are changing the world with new inventions and discoveries — for better and for worse. Breast implants, sex-change operations, and nuclear and chemical weapons are just a few of the widely varying misapplications of knowledge in the brave new world.

Perhaps the most important way in which science is a threat to sanity is in its potential to change the human body. In the past, people used science to manipulate the world outside of the human body; but now the border of the body has been breached; as science is used for plastic surgery, gene manipulation, and organ replacement, our very selves are increasingly being altered. Is someone with silicone in their breasts, an artificial heart, steroid-generated muscle tissue, or a genetically engineered brain still "human" in the sense that we use the term? What if they had all, rather than just one, of those technology-enhanced body parts? Is someone who is kept alive indefinitely on life support systems still really "alive"?

Living Sanely

Many of the most recent scientific innovations have great value, especially in the field of medical technology. The power to repair injury and mitigate disease is truly awesome. Perhaps even more importantly, the nature of work has been changed by technology. Not too long ago, the great majority of work done by humans was the dawn-to-dusk, backbreaking drudgery of agricultural or primitive industrial labor. In the modern age, work is incomparably more interesting — sometimes even enjoyable — and also far more economically rewarding. Because of its impact on health and medical care, standards of living, and ability to make life more interesting, science is generally regarded as a positive force. But we may be at a turning point where science becomes something people fear, partly because of the very fundamental ways in which it is changing the human body. (And also partly due to the ways in which technology is being used to invade privacy.)

If science is to remain a force for positive change, we will need to define what it means to be human. Based on a broad philosophical definition, individuals and organizations need to be selective as to the scientific innovations they pursue.

FOCUS

Not just on whether something can be done,
but whether it should be done.
Is a particular application of science and technology
creating value, or destroying value?

Privacy

"Civilization is the progress toward a society of privacy.
The savage's whole existence is public,
ruled by the laws of the tribe."

— AYN RAND
Russian-American philosopher and novelist, 1905–1982

"Modern Americans are so exposed, peered at, inquired about,
and spied upon as to be increasingly without privacy —
members of a naked society and denizens of a goldfish bowl."

— EDWARD V. LONG
U.S. Senator, 1908–1972

"The right to be alone — the most comprehensive of rights,
and the right most valued by civilized men."

— LOUIS D. BRANDEIS
U.S. Supreme Court Justice, 1856–1941

Insane World

Your phone rings at dinnertime; it's another marketing call; your email box is crammed with unsolicited junk email; most of the mail in your traditional mailbox was generated by a computer. As marketers become increasingly desperate to cut through the clutter (that they have created), the marketing bombardment will only increase. Technology will be used to invade your privacy on a scale previously unimagined: already, computerized systems are leaving automated phone messages, hidden cameras monitor many of your movements, and government and businesses collect and utilize information they have surreptitiously obtained.

Mini-cameras, mini-tape recorders, see-in-the-dark binoculars and a whole host of other equipment originally developed for the military or specialized markets are now being marketed directly to consumers. As technology moves from the laboratory to the masses, almost everyone will have the ability to audiotape, videotape, or otherwise monitor you.

Living Sanely

Privacy is critical to maintaining sanity; the only way to have control over your life is to allocate your attention according to your own priorities, without constant and unsolicited interruption. Determining who is allowed to contact you lets you decide who gets your attention, a very limited resource. In order to control who contacts you, you must control the information about yourself that others receive.

Information about yourself is data that you create; that information is your property. You should provide personal information only in cases where you are confident that it will not be mis-used. Be aware of the potential for invasion of your privacy, and deal ruthlessly with those who are trying to steal your attention. You have no obligation to be polite to those who invade your privacy.

In the future, as the use of mini-cameras and other intrusive technology becomes more widespread, it will make sense to be more vigilant — without being paranoid — about protecting your privacy. You may also want to consider political support of measures designed to curb invasions of privacy.

FOCUS

On controlling the flow of information about yourself,
especially information that allows others to contact you.

Education

"I don't carry information in my mind that is readily available in books. . . . The value of a liberal arts education is that it trains the mind to think. And that's something you can't learn from textbooks."

— ALBERT EINSTEIN
German-American physicist, 1879–1955

"Education is not the taming or domestication of the soul's raw passions — not suppressing them or excising them, which would deprive the soul of its energy — but forming and informing them as art."

— ALLAN BLOOM
American academic and author, 1930–1992

*"The mediocre teacher tells.
The good teacher explains.
The superior teacher demonstrates.
The great teacher inspires."*

— WILLIAM ARTHUR WARD
American evangelist and scholar, living

Insane World

Children begin receiving a formal education when they are three to five years old, and for the next twelve to sixteen years, or longer, they sit in classrooms, read books, and memorize various sorts of data. This process bores or frustrates most of the students most of the time. And what is the end result of all this toil? The number of important facts are far too great for the human brain to retain, and in any event, computers are far better at data retention than human beings.

Yet there are important things that could be gained from formal education — the ability to reason being chief among them. But most students don't acquire reasoning skills. All they typically retain from spending most of their youth in a classroom is some facts they will soon forget, and perhaps, a rudimentary level of skill in math, reading, and writing. A few students also gain basic skills necessary for scientific or technical exploration.

Students also typically acquire some social "skills": The lesson most often retained from formal education may be the value of conformity, both inside and outside the classroom. But this sort of learned conformity is often completely at odds with the kind of independent judgment that is necessary to create value and lead a fulfilling life.

In adult life, people pursue different paths to achieve different goals; there are a wide variety of incentives, including, among others, money, fame, and personal fulfillment. Yet, children are given only the most vague, homogeneous incentive — a message that if they do well in school — memorizing facts that will soon be forgotten — they will do "well" in life.

Living Sanely

Despite the fact that children differ just as much as adults in skills, interests, and potential, formal education offers little variety. A better system would be to let children choose their own path, much as adults do. Before pursuing this path they would have to prove mastery of basic skills in reading, writing, and math, and then, in consultation with their parents, they would be allowed to choose their own course of study. They might finish the most basic course at age eight or age eighteen; and that's a lesson that it's never too early to learn — that people progress at their own rate. All types of students, both the intellectually gifted and otherwise, would have an incentive to finish the basic course so they could pursue their special interests. Such a program would teach one of the most important lessons: You control your own life.

Once students graduate from the basic course they would begin learning another important lesson — the lesson of making life choices. But rather than making these choices in college — after being cast away from family — they could begin to learn these skills while still in a protected environment. The options might be very broad; they could pursue computers and science, sports, mechanical skills, art, working with the disabled, or even leave the school environment completely.

Each citizen could have a number of years of education credit, rather than an age range, during which education would be provided at taxpayer expense. For it is education, rather than youth, that is truly wasted on the young. For example, a student might pass the most basic tests at age thirteen, and then enter specialized training for a trade — perhaps culinary school. At age fifteen they might graduate from culinary school, and then spend seven years as a cook. At that point, after having some exposure to the broader world, he or she might develop an interest in broader education. They might then return to school for the second phase of a more general education. Education, like any other product or service of value, should not be wasted. It should be delivered when it is wanted, and when it will be effective. To be truly effective, education should be integrated into the entire lifespan.

FOCUS

On education as a means of learning to create value.

Life Cycle

"It is never too late to be what you might have been."

— GEORGE ELIOT
English novelist, 1819–1880

"The past cannot be changed. The future is still in your power."

— HUGH LAWSON WHITE
U.S. Senator, 1773–1840

"When I let go of what I am, I become what I might be."

— LAO-TZU
Chinese philosopher and
founder of Taoism, sixth century B.C.

Insane World

Life expectancies are growing rapidly; the average person lived only thirty-seven years at the beginning of the eighteenth century; a child born today will be expected to live more than twice as long. Yet, despite the radical and growing increase in life expectancy, typical life cycles have not changed. We still expect that youth will be devoted to formal education. A male adult will be expected to work from the time he finishes school until he retires, typically around age sixty-five. A woman may follow the same path, or she may leave the work force to raise a family. In a world in which almost everything has changed, little has changed about the typical life cycle.

Despite increasing life expectancies, society still focuses to a very large extent on "youth"; the models for this group are very young athletes and entertainers. But as life expectancies continue to expand, the very idea of "youth" may change. In today's world, someone who is forty years old has probably not even hit the midpoint of his or her life. And as more and more people live to age 100 and beyond, the whole concept of "middle age," "retirement age," and "old age" needs to be re-evaluated.

Living Sanely

A number of factors should have made modern life more flexible and interesting:

- Increased life expectancy.

- A much longer window of opportunity during which men and women can become parents. In modern society, there is nothing uncommon about a man or woman becoming a parent for the first time in their early forties.

- Increased cultural acceptance of alternative lifestyles, including remaining single and childless.

- Increasing overall affluence.

These changes could impact the modern life cycle in a number of positive ways. If a person "retires" at age sixty and is in good health, it is quite likely they will live another twenty to thirty years. Rather than retiring to a life of leisure, they might want to begin a second or third career at this point — one that is based on the personal interests developed during a long life, rather than economic need.

Perhaps the "normal" path for an eighteen year old should be to spend a few years doing simple work, travelling, and generally exploring their options. They'll still have plenty of time left in the future for education and career, and the natural rhythm of life may call for adventure prior to a more settled routine. Perhaps the "normal" time to undertake advanced graduate school education should be at age forty; after one has had a first career, but with plenty of time remaining for a second career. Whether you should try to learn modern dance at age forty or fifty really has more to do with the state of your body than with social mores about the aging process.

FOCUS

Ignore convention;
follow the path that makes sense to you.

Equality and Justice

*"It is the American vice, the democratic disease which expresses its
tyranny by reducing everything unique to the level of the herd."*

— HENRY MILLER
American novelist, 1891–1980

*"It is not true that equality is a law of nature.
Nature knows no equality."*

— LUC DE CLAPIERS, MARQUIS DE VARVENARGUES
French essayist, 1715–1747

*"All men have an equal right to the free development of their
faculties; they have an equal right to the impartial protection of the
state; but it is not true, it is against all the laws of reason and equity,
it is against the eternal nature of things, that the indolent man and
the laborious man, the spendthrift and the economist, the imprudent
and the wise, should obtain and enjoy an equal amount of goods."*

— VICTOR COUSIN
French philosopher, 1792–1867

Insane World

Those who speak of the need for greater equality most often cite the undeniable fact that some people have far more wealth than others. But there are many forms of inequality, of which wealth is only one. There is no evidence that "God," or "the creator," or "nature" ever intended that there be equality, if that term means an equal division of wealth, beauty, intelligence, or any other desirable thing or quality. In other words, there is no reason to think that equality is "natural." If nature intended equality, why is one child born with birth defects, while others are born perfectly healthy? Why will some people grow to be beautiful and others become ugly? Why will some people develop great natural intelligence, while others struggle to keep up? Why do some young people seem to have a natural endowment to become great athletes, while others are prone to obesity or illness?

Living Sanely

The search for some sort of "higher" justice is futile. The whirlwind of human events compounded with the sheer size and diversity of the human race means that there will always be a staggering amount of inequality among people. In keeping with a focus on individuals, you should look for justice not in comparing people to each other, but in assessing the transactions in which they engage. Any transaction between consenting adults that does not involve force or fraud is "just." The test of redressing coercion or fraud is simple: What terms, if any, would have induced the coerced or defrauded party to voluntarily engage in the transaction?

FOCUS

*On the process of honesty and mutual consent,
not on equality of results.*

Art

[Art is] "*A human activity having for its purpose the transmission of the highest and best feelings to which men have risen.*"

— LEO TOLSTOY
Russian novelist, 1828–1910

"*Any young person who has studied Heidegger; or seen Ionesco's 'plays'; or listened to the 'music' of John Cage; or looked at Andy Warhol's 'paintings'— has experienced that feeling of incredulous puzzlement: But this is nonsense! . . . if it made sense, it could be evaluated. The essence of modern intellectual snobbery is the 'emperor's new clothes' approach. Teachers, critics, our self-appointed intellectual elite make it quite clear to us that if we cannot see the superlative nature of this 'art'— why, it merely shows our ignorance, our lack of sophistication and insight. Of course, they go beyond the storybook emperor's tailors, who dressed their victim in nothing and called it fine garments. The modern tailors dress the emperor in garbage.*"

— RON MERRILL
American writer, living

"*When a work lifts your spirits and inspires bold and noble thoughts in you, do not look for any other standard to judge by: the work is good, the product of a master craftsman.*"

— JEAN DE LA BRUYERE
French writer, 1645–1696

Insane World

Visual art is a leading indicator of the way in which society is moving, and one of the most obvious and visible signs that sanity has lost its way. Blank white canvases; photographs of men having sex with each other; paint haphazardly thrown onto a canvas and called art — these are representative of "modern art."

One of the greatest frauds of modern times is the idea that art should be difficult to understand, and that a sign of sophistication and intelligence is understanding what is incomprehensible to the uninitiated. The result is a farce: Those who wish to appear sophisticated pretend to see meaning where there is none.

Living Sanely

Art has a definite purpose: to show what people can and should be. The best art — whether literature, visual, or music — inspires us to be our best. Art is a way of integrating our values; saying in one picture what, as the saying goes, it would take 1,000 words to explain. In this sense, the best art affects us in an immediate and emotionally captivating way. Great art reaffirms our most important values; mediocre art confuses; bad art degrades us. The best art lifts us up; the worst art shows contempt for the idea that there is any "up."

FOCUS

Find art that inspires you to be your best self.

Entertainment and the Media

*"Nurture your mind with great thoughts;
to believe in the heroic makes heroes."*

— BENJAMIN DISRAELI
British Prime Minister, 1804–1881

*"Wars, famine, crime, violence, inflation, recession,
a shifting of traditional forms of social interaction,
the threat of nuclear proliferation, HIV, holocaust in
all its horrific forms, are all communicated instantly
and continuously to the fixated consumer,
to all of us watching TV."*

— MICHAEL GERBER
American business writer

*"To a philosopher all 'news,' as it is called, is gossip,
and they who edit and read it are old women over their tea."*

— HENRY DAVID THOREAU
American writer and poet, 1817–1862

Insane World

People have the chance to live, but they spend most of their time living through others. Movie stars become famous by pretending to be other people, and real people fantasize about the lives of movie stars. Entertainers of all types — sports figures, musicians, television stars — are worshipped from the couch. Meanwhile, never in human history has there been more opportunity for individuals to live for themselves, and never have so many people had so much disposable income to take advantage of those opportunities. Yet they don't. Life is not a spectator sport and can't be lived to its fullest through the sifted vision of others.

Perhaps even more disturbing than the secondhand nature of media and entertainment is the twisted perspective on life that the media provides. Most people's lives are rarely, if ever, touched by murder, rape, or robbery, but in the nightly news, violence and tragedy are daily, commonplace events.

Living Sanely

The real world is a much more positive place than the world portrayed in the media. When evaluating the state of the world, one question to ask is, "How often do the events portrayed on the news happen to me or people that I know?"

Further, the people and events that attract media interest — wars, violence, celebrities — are not the forces – such as science and technology — that really change the world. News has become entertainment, rather than information that will help guide your actions. It's difficult to create value without being a keen observer of the world around you, and in order to accurately observe and assess that world, you have to constantly seek an accurate picture of reality. But the best way to observe the world is firsthand, as a participant — through travel, work, and interaction with different kinds of people — not through the twisted filter of the media.

FOCUS

Perceive and assess reality directly,
through your own experience and judgment,
rather than relying on the portrayal
of the world as presented by the media.

Celebrity

"To live in the presence of great truths and eternal laws, to be led by permanent ideals - that is what keeps a man patient when the world ignores him, and calm and unspoiled when the world praises him."

— HONORÉ DE BALZAC
French novelist, 1799–1850

"One's true happiness depends more upon one's own judgment of one's self, on a consciousness of rectitude in action and intention, and in the approbation of those few who judge impartially, than upon the applause of the unthinking undiscerning multitude, who are apt to cry 'Hosanna' today, and tomorrow, 'crucify him.'"

— BENJAMIN FRANKLIN
American statesman, 1706–1790

"The work an unknown good man has done is like a vein of water flowing hidden underground, secretly making the ground green."

— THOMAS CARLYLE
Scottish writer, 1795–1881

Insane World

People doing important work in science, technology, business, and many other fields live in obscurity while the most trivial but visible work leads to fame. Actors become more famous than the people they portray while television "personalities" become more famous than the people they interview. The element most likely to lead to fame is not accomplishment, talent, or merit, but simply visibility through the media.

The public avidly follows the lives of celebrities, no matter how banal or senseless those lives might be. The distinction between fame and infamy has been lost as visibility, rather than moral worth, becomes the criteria for determining who is "celebrated." The most visible people, such as athletes and entertainers, tend to have the least long-term impact, while people toiling in obscurity in laboratories or on college campuses are the driving forces behind profound changes in society.

Living Sanely

Visibility and fame do not equal importance. Having portrayed a person of merit in a drama is not the same as being a person of merit. And, conversely, obscurity has no relationship to unimportance.

Pay attention to those who are worthy of your attention, regardless of whether those people are celebrities or unknown. Who is worthy of your attention, and perhaps, emulation or admiration? Those who are creating value.

FOCUS

On the difference between fame and worth.

Drugs and Alcohol

"As a cure for worrying, work is better than whiskey."

— THOMAS A. EDISON
American inventor, 1847–1931

*"Better keep yourself clean and bright;
you are the window through which you must see the world."*

— GEORGE BERNARD SHAW
Irish playwright, 1856–1950

*"I searched through rebellion, drugs, diets, mysticism,
religions, intellectualism and much more, only to begin to find . . .
that truth is basically simple — and feels good, clean, and right."*

— CHICK COREA
American Jazz musician, 1941–NA

Insane World

Many people use drugs and/or alcohol to escape the insanity of modern life. People who don't have goals, and who aren't busy trying to create value in some form, often use drugs to escape boredom.

As science and technology increase their impact on modern life, the opportunities for chemical escapism will increase. One vision of the future is found in Aldous Huxley's *Brave New World*, where the soma drug provides the escape of an almost endless dream. In the short-term, mind-altering drugs offer many attractions: sensual stimulation, intense experience, escape from worry and trouble. The long-term effects are not so enchanting, as drug use typically leaves the users wasted and spent, in many cases a pathetic shell of their former selves. Long-term drug use often causes permanent physical or mental damage.

Living Sanely

Of course there is a role for pain-killing drugs in modern medicine, and for moderate alcohol use that does not impair the user physically or mentally. And, contrary to public propaganda, there appears to be little permanent harm from short-term, experimental use of "recreational" drugs such as marijuana. But there are many reasons why those seeking to live sanely should severely limit their use of drugs and alcohol:

- Reason is your primary, and often only, weapon of self-defense, and mind-altering drugs can leave you defenseless.

- Drugs are not an aid to creative work of lasting value.

- You can ruin your life with one major mistake: A car accident, a loss of temper that leads to violence, or simply saying something that would be better left unsaid. You are far more likely to make such a mistake under the influence of drugs or alcohol.

Most fundamentally, living sanely requires that your life has integrity, an overarching context, and that you continually make your best assessment of facts and reality. To live your life in this sort of integrated way requires that you never lose self-control or your capacity to think clearly.

FOCUS

Sobriety helps you maintain your ability to focus on the long-term, think clearly, and accurately assess reality.

Chance and Reason

"Nothing splendid has ever been achieved except by those who dared believe that something inside them was superior to circumstances."

— BRUCE FAIRCHILD BARTON
American advertising executive, 1886–1967

"People are always blaming their circumstances for what they are. I don't believe in circumstances. The people who get on in this world are the people who get up and look for the circumstances they want, and, if they can't find them, make them."

— GEORGE BERNARD SHAW
Irish playwright, 1856–1950

"Life is not holding a good hand; life is playing a poor hand well."

— DANISH PROVERB

Insane World

Success seems to be as much a matter of luck as of character. A lucky number drawn in a lottery, and instantly, the winner is rich. A chance opportunity, and suddenly someone's career takes off. Insane jury verdicts seem like lotteries and wrongly result in great wealth for some, great loss for others, freedom for some, and imprisonment for others. Being in the wrong place at the wrong time leads to injury or death from accident or the whim of some deranged terrorist.

Living Sanely

Luck or chance plays a large role in life, but no role in how you should live your life. You can live sanely, even in an insane world. The key is to focus on your own actions, over which you have great control. Regard other people, and the world in general, as something completely separate from yourself: part of nature that you accept as is, in the same way you accept the fact that the sun rises and the winds blow.

Reason should be your guiding force, but if you expect reason from others you will be sorely disappointed, and you will waste much time in despair. Make the most rational decisions possible, taking into account those factors that are predictable, and knowing that there may be factors outside of your control. Realize that you can control your own actions, but not the actions of others.

Part of living sanely is choosing not to do things, like playing the lottery, that completely depend on chance or luck. While it's true that lotteries have "winners," the vast majority of players lose, and overall, lotteries are a poor investment. In other words, for the rational investor, the expected return is negative. More importantly:

- Sanity requires a consistent reliance on reason, rather than occasional blind faith in luck. Like ethics, reason is not a matter of whim or convenience; it must be in constant use to work.

- Sane people don't want to succeed through luck or chance; they want to succeed by creating value.

- In terms of keeping score with yourself, money won through chance has no value.

Never confuse irrational gambling with calculated risk-taking. Almost every aspect of life involves risk — from falling in love to buying a house to running a business. The sane way of dealing with risk is to carefully calculate the risks and rewards and then to use your best judgment. You will often make the wrong decision, but on balance, decisions made in this way will guide your life in the best direction.

You may fail due to unforeseeable events or errors of your best judgment. Success matters very much, but it is a desired outcome of rational decisions, rather than something one actually controls.

FOCUS

On making rational decisions for yourself,
while not expecting reason from others.

Honesty

*"The true hypocrite is the one who ceases to perceive his deception,
the one who lies with sincerity."*

— ANDRÉ GIDE
French writer, 1869–1951

*"Happiness is when what you think, what you say,
and what you do are in harmony."*

— MAHATMA GANDHI
Indian nationalist, 1869–1948

*"The first virtue of all really great men is that they are sincere.
They eradicate hypocrisy from their hearts."*

— ANATOLE FRANCE
French novelist, 1844–1924

Insane World

Honesty is, in theory, universally regarded as an important virtue, but is generally practiced only sporadically. Within certain professions, such as politics or the law, blatant dishonesty is so fundamental as to be taken for granted. In business, especially in consumer advertising, exaggeration and hyperbole are everyday facts of life. Throughout society, the desire to create the most favorable impression, or to promote a product, an idea, or a person, has created a cultural acceptance of "spinning" the truth that is so prevalent, it often goes unnoticed.

Living Sanely

Honesty is the primary moral virtue, from which other virtues flow. The principle rule in dealing with adults is mutual consent, and the combination of mutual consent and honesty eliminates the two primary types of unethical action: force and fraud.

Honesty is often inconvenient and forces us to take a more difficult path, but, in the long run, the more difficult path is often the one that leads us in the most fulfilling direction. In other words, the quickest way to end up doing what you really should be doing is to be as honest as possible in all important matters. Being honest with yourself and others will often lead to temporary setbacks, or even to acknowledging occasional failure, but it will force you to make what are, in the long run, the best choices.

Caution: Honesty in the important intercourse of life is critical, but trivial matters may be better governed by rules of courtesy.

FOCUS

By being honest with yourself and others,
you do the right thing,
and also what is ultimately in your best interests.

Stealing

"Duty . . . is not what a lawyer tells me I may do;
but what humanity, reason,
and justice tell me I ought to do."

— EDMUND BURKE
British political philosopher, 1729–1797

"It has been far safer to steal large sums
with a pen than small sums with a gun."

— WARREN BUFFETT
American investor, 1930–NA

"Unnecessary laws are not good laws, but traps for money."

— THOMAS HOBBES
English philosopher, 1588–1679

Insane World

Taking things that do not rightfully belong to one is stealing, and it has many forms in the modern world, some of them quite legal:

- *Taxation:* A complex, institutionalized form of stealing whereby the mechanisms of government are used to take wealth from those who create value and transfer it to those who apply political pressure. For most Americans, this form of extortion — you pay your taxes or go to jail — is their single biggest expense, often taking half of their total income in the form of income tax, sales tax, property tax, Social Security tax, Medicare tax, and myriad other types of taxation. This type of stealing is tolerated because it is traditional, institutionalized, and because so many people believe they benefit from it. Once the government steals through taxation, it can redistribute money in myriad forms, from welfare for the poor to subsidies for huge corporations.

- *Intellectual property theft:* Otherwise honest people routinely steal intellectual property such as writing, music, software, or visual art. Often such intellectual property, supposedly protected by copyright law, is thoughtlessly copied, without permission and without compensation to the person who created the work. Most people view this type of stealing as harmless because it does not involve tangible goods.

- *Civil litigation:* The fastest growing form of theft has been aided by the fact that there is virtually no limit to the types of "injury" for which one can demand compensation: racial discrimination, product liability, sexual harassment — the list is endless. Damage awards, like the ability of lawyers to emotionally manipulate juries, are unlimited.

- *Insurance fraud:* Whenever unethical people see a great pool of money, they grab for it. The types of insurance fraud are as varied as the types of insurance, with inflated injury claims from automobile accidents leading the list. Often the injury is invented; other times the loss is exaggerated, but wherever insurance exists, so does significant insurance fraud.

- *Divorce:* When a marriage breaks up because of divorce, assets are not divided according to who created value. For instance, in states in which community property laws apply, all wealth created since the marriage is divided evenly, even if one spouse created all the wealth while another simply spent it. In other cases, if one provides a luxurious lifestyle for their spouse, they also incur an obligation to maintain that lifestyle if they divorce. This is true even if they divorce because the person they treated so generously made them miserable.

- *Abuse of philanthropy:* Private philanthropy comes in many forms, ranging from the impulsive generosity of individuals to the structured giving of foundations. Much of what is given with the best of intentions seems to be misused or abused by the recipients.

- *Petty theft:* Minor theft, such as using an employer's phone to avoid paying for a personal call, or taking a towel or ashtray from a hotel, is still theft.

Living Sanely

Self-respect requires that you clearly determine what is rightfully yours and what is not. This is not done in order to protect others, but to protect yourself from corruption of the soul. The question to ask is not, "Can I get away with it," but "Do I have a right to this?" Whether others can afford to take a loss is irrelevant — either you have a right to something or you don't. As always, your interest should be selfish: Enhancing your character and staying on the path that will lead you to create value and fulfill your potential.

FOCUS

On earning money commensurate with the value you create.

Ethics

"In matters of style, swim with the current;
in matters of principle, stand like a rock."

— THOMAS JEFFERSON
Third U.S. President, 1743–1826

"We can often do more for other men by trying to correct
our own faults than by trying to correct theirs."

— FRANÇOIS FÉNELON
French Roman Catholic theologian, 1651–1715

"Goodness is a special kind of truth and beauty.
It is truth and beauty in human behavior."

— H. A. OVERSTREET
American author

Insane World

Everyone talks about ethics and doing the right thing, and these ideas are, in fact, important to most people. But power and wealth often flow to those who show the least regard for ethical considerations; the most ruthless dictators often attain unlimited power, and modern democracies are governed by politicians whose ruling passion seems to be hypocrisy. There appears to be no correlation between wealth and goodness — often the wealthiest people have little or no regard for ethics.

Living Sanely

The most interesting question is not what ethical standards should be — virtues, especially the value of honesty, are generally intuitive and widely acknowledged. The most interesting question is, "Do ethics matter?" In other words, if you know the right thing, why should you do it?

At one time, when almost all Europeans and North Americans subscribed to the doctrines of conventional religion, the answer to this question was simpler: If you did the right thing, you would go to Heaven and enjoy eternal bliss; do the wrong thing and you were destined for the endless tortures of Hell. But if you judge ethics in the context of life on earth, the answer becomes less obvious.

But ethics do matter, and serve important functions:

- To simplify decision-making. When evaluating alternative actions, ones that are wrong should simply be eliminated from consideration, leaving only those options that are morally acceptable.

- To lead you to your most fulfilling destiny. It is impossible for any man or woman to look into the future and predict the long-term consequences of a series of actions. In each situation, by doing the right thing, you advance in the direction that is best for you, even if you cannot see or know the full, long-term implications of your actions or how those actions ultimately affect your life.

- To make a comprehensible game of life, in the grandest sense. To keep score, you must have a set of rules. But the rules are only effective if you believe in them: they must be rules you create — not a set of rules which are dictated to you.

- To evaluate the actions of others. The most important role of ethics is to judge your own actions — which you can control — rather than to judge others. But you do need to decide whom to associate with, whom to do business with, whom to love; all of these relationships will be more successful if you choose people with ethical values similar to your own.

- You may be called to sit on a jury; you certainly have a responsibility to vote; in these situations the ability to exercise moral judgment is imperative. The standard should hark back to yourself; you should judge others by standards no more or less demanding than your own. When judging others, it may be useful to ask, "If I had committed this action, what judgment would I regard as fair?"

What separates ethics from other elements in life is that ethics require rigid adherence, unlike other areas in which compromise is often proper and feasible. Compromised ethics are really no ethics at all — the ethics of convenience are meaningless.

Ethics means drawing a firm line between the things you will and will not do to reach your objectives. And to take ethics seriously is to say that process is more important than results, rather than vice versa.

FOCUS

On ethics as a positive part of your personal philosophy that can help you create value and reach your full potential as a human being.

Selfishness

"Only a rationally selfish man, a man of self-esteem, is capable of love — because he is the only man capable of holding firm, consistent, uncompromising, unbetrayed values. The man who does not value himself, cannot value anything or anyone."

— AYN RAND
Russian-American philosopher and novelist, 1905–1982

"The greatest productive force is human selfishness."

— ROBERT HEINLEIN
American science fiction writer, 1907–1988

"It is easy to live for others; everybody does. I call on you to live for yourselves."

— RALPH WALDO EMERSON
American poet and essayist, 1803–1882

Insane World

Any action which benefits myself is selfish, and thus not very virtuous, while any action I do for the benefit of someone else is unselfish, and thus good. Nothing could be more perverse, in that living for oneself is as natural to a man or woman as eating or breathing. Yet because it's generally accepted that self-interest is bad, people go through all sorts of contortions to represent their selfish actions as being motivated by concern for others.

Living Sanely

The great mistake that is commonly made is to define one's interest exclusively, or even primarily, in material terms. Self-interest can take many forms. It may be in my short-term interest to see a child laugh, as I derive pleasure from the sight. It may be in my long-term interest to build a great business, for reasons that have little to do with material reward. It may be in my selfish interest to give away money if I think I'm creating value with the gift.

Not only is living selfishly natural, it is also rational. In order to make choices, one must make value judgments, and you can only make value judgments based on your own values. In other words, it is impossible to create value without defining value (perhaps only intuitively), but that definition must be based on your own view of reality. Even a person who is completely devoted to someone else has a very difficult time determining what is really in the other person's best interests, which is one reason why raising children is so difficult.

FOCUS

*On seeking your own interests based on
a broad, long-term perspective.*

Helping Others

"I am only one; but still I am one. I cannot do everything, but still I can do something; I will not refuse to do the something I can do."

— HELEN KELLER
American writer, 1880–1968

"Blessed are those who can give without remembering and take without forgetting."

— ELIZABETH ASQUITH BIBESCO
English writer, 1897–1945

"Do not wait for leaders; do it alone, person to person."

— MOTHER TERESA
Albanian missionary, 1910–1997

Insane World

Actions are judged on their intent, rather than on results. This leads to a bizarre world in which the actions of governments, individuals, and not-for-profit organizations are often governed by good intentions, even when good intentions generate disastrous results. (A classic example is the "We Are The World" music recordings performed by leading American pop artists in the 1980s to help the victims of Ethiopian famine. In fact, the money was used by the rulers of Ethiopia to buy weapons.)

Living Sanely

Intentions matter, but so do results. The desire to help others is not a guarantee that an action is worthwhile. Well-intentioned actions that generate poor results are not worthy of praise. Those who seek to help others should follow the ancient creed of the medical profession: First, do no harm.

Despite these cautions, there are occasions when providing some form of assistance may create value. The keys to creating value through charity are:

- The recipient must be a fundamentally good person who is worthy of assistance.

- Desire and motivation cannot be given; the recipient must have the drive to succeed.

- Help should be temporary; it should enable the recipients to move forward on their own.

- The recipient must desire and agree to be helped, and not resent or be embittered by assistance.

- The donor must have a genuine desire to help, rather than to appear virtuous to others.

If all of these criteria are met, helping others can be an extremely rewarding experience. Possible worthy recipients are unfortunately unlimited and might include an abused child, a handicapped adult, a struggling artist, a family seeking freedom from an oppressive political system, or many others. Help might be in the form of money, contacts, information, guidance — again, the list is endless. But one common thread is that no matter who the recipient is or what form the aid takes, the most valuable component is often the reassurance that comes from knowing that someone else cares enough to help.

FOCUS

Are your efforts to help others actually helping them?
How can you help others create value?

Legal System

"When wrongs are pressed because it is believed they will be borne, resistance becomes morality."

— THOMAS JEFFERSON
Third U.S. President, 1743–1826

"He that's merciful to the bad is cruel to the good."

— THOMAS RANDOLPH
English poet and playwright, 1605–1635

"It is not desirable to cultivate a respect for the law, so much as for the right."

— HENRY DAVID THOREAU
American philosopher, 1817–1862

Insane World

The legal system is driven by politics and the greed of lawyers, not justice. There is nothing profound about the way that laws are made: Politicians respond to interest group pressure to advance their political careers, occasionally modifying their actions based on political principle. Lawyers sue anyone on any pretext of getting a large, or huge, contingency fee. Bureaucrats swamp businesses with countless layers of Byzantine regulation.

The criminal justice system is completely arbitrary, and depends more on the political climate of the times and the craftiness of lawyers than on the nature of the crime committed. A famous athlete may knife two people to death and go free, even with overwhelming evidence against him, by taking advantage of racial animosity. Another man may walk into his brother's home, kill him with a shotgun, and serve less than three years in prison. On the other hand, many people serve long jail sentences for victimless crimes such as possession or sale of drugs. Part of the problem with the modern legal system is that it is very unpredictable, as it relies so heavily on the irrational judgments of legislators, judges, and juries.

The prison population increases, but no more justice seems to be done. The death penalty is rarely implemented, due to lack of confidence in the system and misplaced sympathy for criminals.

Living Sanely

One key to sanity is to keep expectations low. Another key is, to the extent possible, to avoid working in highly regulated businesses. Avoid the court system when possible, but never compromise on matters of principle. Base your decisions on your own sense of right and wrong, and hope that judges and juries will agree. If your judgment of right and wrong differs from the law, then the critical question is purely utilitarian — will you be subject to punishment if you do what you think is right? In such cases, if you are confident you will escape punishment, you should break the law. The noblest people break the law even when they know they will be caught and severely punished, because they have the most inviolable sense of personal morality.

The idea behind democracy is that you have the power to elect politicians who will represent your views of right and wrong, and implement proper safeguards for individual liberty. In a working democracy, you should not have to take the law into your own hands; you should leave the implementation of justice to the legal system. But when society has gone insane — when the most fundamental concepts of common sense and right and wrong are lost, you have both a right and a responsibility to implement justice in the sphere of your own life.

In some cases, behavior that appears to be destructive may actually create value. A rational, thoughtful effort to implement justice can have far more value than commonly lauded virtues such as forgiveness or leniency, which are often motivated by fear or the desire to forget. As a general rule, people that are truly evil will always be evil, and imprisoning or killing such a person may prevent their committing crimes against other innocent people. To destroy what is evil is often to protect what is good.

FOCUS

First, decide what is right.
Secondly, look at the law in purely mechanical terms — what
is the price of doing the right thing, and is it worth it?

The Value of Life

"If a man hasn't discovered something that he would die for,
he isn't fit to live."

— MARTIN LUTHER KING, JR.
American civil rights leader, 1929–1968

"No one knows but that death is the greatest of all good to man;
yet men fear it, as if they well knew that it is the greatest of evils.
Is not this the more reprehensible ignorance,
to think that one knows what one does not know?"

— SOCRATES
Athenian philosopher, 470 B.C.–399 B.C.

"There is but one truly serious philosophical problem,
and that is suicide. Judging whether life is or is not
worth living amounts to answering
the fundamental question of philosophy."

— ALBERT CAMUS
French writer, 1913–1960

Insane World

When people discuss the sanctity of life, and issues such as abortion and the death penalty, they seem to imply that human life has a fixed and unchanging value, and that everyone's life has the same high value. But does all human life have the same value? Hardly; in fact, many lives, by the choice of those who live them, have little or no value — to themselves or others.

Many people passionately oppose the killing of a convicted criminal, while passionately defending the right to kill an innocent fetus. Juries award astronomical judgments to the families of those killed by accident, often making the victim far more valuable dead than alive. Suicide is discouraged and sometimes illegal, although the uncertainty of death may be preferable to the certainty of a miserable life.

Living Sanely

In order to create value, one must be prepared to make value judgments. Most often, these judgments focus on your own actions, but one must also be prepared to judge others. There are five types of situations in which you might have to make the ultimate judgment regarding the value of an individual life:

- Capital Punishment: Not only does the life of a serial rapist or a murderer have no value, but they seek to destroy the value they find in others. Yet, no matter how terrible the crime, or beyond redemption the criminal, there are many who believe that "mercy" is always the appropriate course of action, and that fallible men have no right to take a human life. I disagree. If one is sure that a criminal has committed a crime worthy of death, it is absolutely just to kill the criminal, preferably through the workings of the criminal justice system, but if necessary and feasible, through private action. The range of crimes necessitating the death penalty might include, under certain circumstances: murder, rape, or, if on a massive scale, stealing. One can create value by ridding society of value-destroyers.

Under certain rare circumstances, even assassination can be a form of value creation. How many millions of lives would have been saved if Hitler, Mao, or Stalin had been killed before they had the chance to destroy others?

- Abortion: This is a very complex and difficult issue. The producers of the child, the parents, have created something of great potential — a fetus. The parents have an obligation to make sure that this life has the chance to reach its potential, without destroying the value already created in the parents' life. To simply add one more human life to the billions that already exist is meaningless; to create or destroy value is very meaningful. For an unplanned child, the parents must make a very difficult choice — or a choice that should be very difficult: Provide the tremendous amount of time, effort, and affection necessary to help the baby reach its potential, without destroying the parents' own life, or destroy the fetus.

- Wrongful death: You may be a member of a jury judging a wrongful death case, or have some other occasion for deciding what reparations should be made regarding death caused by the wrongful actions of others, or perhaps by yourself. In many cases, monetary compensation is not appropriate — life and death should not be treated as commercial transactions. In cases in which financial compensation is appropriate, I would argue that the range of appropriate "compensation" is as wide as life itself. Compensation for a life that was not being enjoyed, or was not useful to others, might be quite low. Conversely, compensation for a life full of potential might be extremely high. In any event, someone should not be worth more dead than alive.

Compensation for death is made more complex by the fact that the most aggrieved person, the one who died, obviously cannot receive any benefit from the award.

- Suicide: While struggling to survive against adversity is one of the noblest things a person can do, this should not blind us to the fact that biological life, in and of itself, has no value. Life only has value if a person can live in a manner acceptable to them. And it is only because life is a finite thing — that it has an ending — that makes it valuable. There is a time to die, and that time is when you can no longer live life your own way. There are many situations in which voluntary death may be more acceptable than life — medical incapacity being the most obvious. Life on a life support system is not life worth living. But there may also be other circumstances in which death is preferable to life. Only the person considering suicide can make this ultimate decision.

We're always afraid of the unknown, and we don't know what happens to us when we die. But isn't the unknown to be preferred to an unbearable life? The highest level of control of one's destiny is to choose the time of death. Sooner or later, voluntarily or involuntarily, everyone must confront death.

• The ultimate sacrifice: On very rare occasions a person with much to live for may choose to die to save the life of someone they love — or a stranger. This scenario is most likely in wartime or in an emergency. Such situations usually require extremely fast decisions, but before risking your own life, you will hopefully have a chance to decide if the person you are trying to save is worthy of the ultimate sacrifice.

For the hero, death may simply be a natural extension of life. You may be called to choose between danger to your life and the danger of sacrificing that part of yourself which you value most highly — the heroic soul. It is probably more rational to risk your life than to risk your self-esteem.

FOCUS

Value other people's lives using the same criteria you use to value your own life.

Perspective

"I wept because I had no shoes, until I saw a man who had no feet."

— ANCIENT PERSIAN PROVERB

*"Despite some of the horrors and barbarisms of modern life
which appall and grieve us, life has — or has the potential of —
such richness, joy and adventure as were unknown
to our ancestors except in their dreams."*

— ARTHUR H. COMPTON
American physicist, 1892–1962

*"People call me an optimist, but I'm really an appreciator. . . .
When I was six years old and had scarlet fever,
the first of the miracle drugs, sulfanilamide, saved my life.
I'm grateful for computers and photocopiers . . .
I appreciate where we've come from."*

— JULIAN SIMON
American academic, 1933–1998

Insane World

The bored rich seek therapy for their lack of contentment while millions of people around the world don't have enough to eat. Workers with good jobs in rich countries file lawsuits against their employers for all sorts of trivial grievances, while countless people around the globe are desperate to find any sort of paying labor. Rich and famous athletes and entertainers moan that they're not adequately "appreciated." The paradox of the modern age is that never have so many had so much – and complained so often.

Living Sanely

Generally, this guide encourages you to focus on yourself, and not compare yourself with others, but there is a broad sense of perspective that you need to maintain both sanity and common sense. This perspective falls into two broad categories: the past and the present.

The Past: For the great majority of the time mankind has roamed planet earth, life has been short, hard, and, dull. As late as the eighteenth century, the average life expectancy in Europe and North America was less than forty years — it is now almost twice as long. Until the twentieth century, infant mortality was very high, and parents could expect the heartbreak of seeing some, even most, of their children die before reaching adulthood. In the past, the typical workday was very long and consisted of mind-numbingly dull agricultural labor. The general standard of living for both rich and poor was far lower than it is today. Educational, recreational, and cultural activities were far more limited, and effective medical care was practically non-existent.

The Present: Even with the great progress that has been made over time, those of us living in counties with established democratic, free-market systems are still far better off than those who live in countries emerging from despotic regimes and controlled economies. Millions of people around the world still lack the most basic of life's necessities. Even with the amazing innovations in medical science, millions still battle serious physical handicaps or crippling disease, even in the most technologically advanced countries.

In addition to appreciating the general economic and scientific advances that make our lives relatively comfortable and easy, we should keep our day-to-day challenges in perspective. Even in rich, technologically advanced countries, every hour of every day some people face rape, accidental death, complete ruin, or some other genuine tragedy. We should appreciate the fact that our daily struggle is, generally, not life-threatening.

FOCUS

*On appreciating the advantages of modern life in
a free society, and not mistaking challenges for tragedies.*

"This shall be the new light, the new sun,
which rises when the worn-out one shall set,
and shall give light to them who are in shadow and darkness
because of the old sun, which did not enlighten them."

— DANTE ALIGHIERI
De Vulgari Eloquentia

115

Index